Dear Kale

And Other Letters I Wrote to (Mostly) Inanimate Objects

ROMI BRENNER

ISBN: 0-9798749-3-9
ISBN-13: 978-0-9798749-3-2

Book Cover Design by Deborah Bradseth of
Tugboat Design

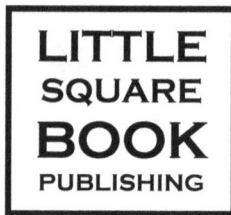

**LITTLE
SQUARE
BOOK
PUBLISHING**

www.littlesquarebook.com

Dedicated to my beloved father, who left us far too soon. I miss you Dad, and I'm *still* your little girl.

CONTENTS

DEAR GROCERY STORE CART WITH THE FIRE TRUCK ON THE FRONT

Dear Grocery Store Cart with the Fire Truck on the Front,

I know the person who designed you probably had the best of intentions. I know they probably thought you would help keep little ones occupied while their parents go through the arduous chore that to childless people is known as shopping, but to all those with tiny people in tow is known as the seventh layer of hell.

Grocery Store Cart with the Fire Truck on the Front, the problem is that, to begin with, you are usually already taken. This results in a small meltdown before we've even got inside the door because all that's left is the police car, the pink car or the taxi. (Unless of course it's the police car that my child wants, in which case you are always available, and it isn't. But I digress.)

My next beef with you is that you're so, so, so loooong. You are impossible to maneuver and require a twelve-point turning nightmare, moving back and forth with more precision than is needed by the NASA team to reenter the earth's atmosphere, just to round the corner to go down an aisle. People have legs, Grocery Store Cart with the Fire Truck on the Front, and I end up unintentionally ramming you into the backs of them. As you can imagine this does NOT endear me to my fellow shoppers.

The other thing Grocery Store Cart with the Fire Truck on the Front, while really more my problem than yours, is that approximately fifty seconds after buckling himself into the cart, my boy escapes from his shackles and dashes off down the aisle anyway. Then I am stuck with you for no good reason, and am forced to try and weave your behemoth cage throughout the crowd as I dash after my child, hissing at him like a crazed feral cat to COME BACK HERE AND GET BACK IN THE CART! RIGHT! NOW!

The other thing I need to address with you is the small problem of my boy pulling random things I don't need off the shelves and throwing them inside your cart compartment. For a while I would actually push you down the very middle of the aisle, trying to keep little octopus arms from swiping all sorts of loot from the sides as I swept each row. But every so often I'd have to pull to the side to let some other shopper go past and then the pilfering would occur, within seconds. After looking at the toothpastes one afternoon, I turned my attention back to my son to find him clutching a box of tampons under his arm.

I tried to gently pull the box away from his vice-like grip, only to be reprimanded very loudly.

"MINE!" He shrieked, holding onto the box even more tightly. There were a few subsequent attempts to get him to release the box but they were sadly unsuccessful. My son and his tampons were not to be separated until we got to the checkout at which point the box was so crushed that although this wasn't even the brand I use, I felt obliged to buy them.

But it's a double-edged sword, Grocery Store Cart with the Fire Truck on the Front. I cringe when I see that you're available and I cringe when I don't. This just won't end well for me either way.

I honestly don't know whether to wish for your demise or hope for more like you.

In a quandary,
Romi

DEAR TUESDAY

Dear Tuesday,

I thought I should let you know I feel bad for you. You are just a... well... nothing day.

Monday is the bad boy that everybody hates. It comes along swiftly and totally destroys the weekend bliss. There are posts dedicated to Monday on Facebook, songs about the Monday blahs. Even when other days are not going well, people will say "that was a real Monday Thursday" or "that was the Monday-est Wednesday ever," etc.

Monday's reputation precedes it. It's the anti-day, the villain of the week; the day everyone loves to hate. But at least it sparks an emotion, even if it's negative.

Wednesday is hump day, the day that signals it's halfway over, that people just need to hang in there for a few more days and they will be rewarded with another weekend. Wednesday is the point in the marathon where you realize you have run more than you have left to run. It inspires you to keep going. Wednesday is the perfect cheerleader.

People like Thursday because it's only a day away from the most popular day of all. For some who take a long three day weekend, it IS their Friday. Thursday is the part of the marathon when you're ready to collapse, but then see you only have one last mile to go so you find it within yourself to keep going.

Then comes Friday, and everyone is in serious party mode. Even all the crap that goes wrong at four thirty in the afternoon once everyone else has gone home for the day doesn't seem to bother people. Things like the "system breaking down," or someone desperately needing your help for a "very, very, very urgent issue that CANNOT wait" until the following week, or to provide a last minute analysis on some metric that has the same level of importance as whether or not belly button lint can be harvested for a new energy efficient power source.

It all simply doesn't matter anymore, because it's Friday, and people are so checked out and mentally already at their parties and dancing on tables at local bars that they just don't care, or are happy to oblige just to get out of there and get the weekend underway.

And then of course, there's Saturday. What can I say. There is no competing with Saturday and there never will be. The sky's the limit and what happens on Saturday stays on Saturday. You can always sleep it off on Sunday.

Sunday is more somber than Saturday because of course it signals the end of the weekend, for those who aren't too hung over to remember it, and the day before the dreaded worst day of all.

But you, Tuesday? You are nothing but Monday's insipid apprentice. You just come and go studiously without anyone really noticing. This is the day where everyone is working hard and doing their thing; there is no oomph for you. All I can really say about you is that many deals must be made on Tuesdays; I'm sure people know it's one of the few days where folks can actually get anything done.

I imagine that's probably a small consolation for being so lackluster. Thanks for carrying the week, Tuesday. *I* think you're awesome. Maybe when you get reincarnated you can come back as Friday or something?

Hang in there, friend,
Romi

DEAR KABOCHA SQUASH THAT

EXPLODED IN THE OVEN

Dear Kabocha Squash that Exploded in the Oven,
Well, who knew?

In my defense, I didn't realize you had to puncture a squash before putting it in the oven. I thought that was just for microwaves. I, er, am not the most domesticated of goddesses. Obviously.

I do have to say though, when the force of your detonation actually flung the oven door open, literally throwing my two hundred and twenty pound, six foot four husband backwards, it was quite impressive. I almost laughed honestly, until I saw the ensuing blast of steam that nearly singed the poor man's eyebrows off, effectively squelching the peals of hysteria that were threatening to bubble up out of my mouth, thereby rescuing me from undoubtedly making the situation much, much worse.

It was quite the expletive-fest as you can imagine, Kabocha Squash that Exploded in the Oven. He was far less amused than I.

Once the oven had cooled sufficiently we returned to the wreckage, and it was sheer carnage. Oh Kabocha Squash that Exploded in the Oven. Your beautifully rounded form was burst open. There were strands and chunks of your precious innards all over the oven; strewn through the racks like a gruesome vegetable murder scene.

We had peas that night, Kabocha Squash that Exploded in the Oven.

I'm so, so sorry.

Romi

DEAR T-SHIRT THAT THE GOAT
STARTED CHEWING AT THE ZOO

Dear T-Shirt That the Goat Started Chewing at the Zoo,

It started innocently enough. Our extended family was in town so we thought we'd take the kids to the zoo. It was a beautiful day; the azure sky uninterrupted by even a single wisp of cloud. I wore you for two reasons: I knew your light, cotton composition would keep me cool as the temperature climbed, and the brilliance of your deep jewel-toned turquoise would work nicely with my complexion (thank you!).

We were going to have it all that day, T-Shirt That the Goat Started Chewing at the Zoo. And indeed, the first few hours passed with the ease one would expect from a fun trip to the zoo: a little walking, a lot of gawking, a snack here and there

Then, we got to the petting zoo. I don't like the petting zoo, T-Shirt That the Goat Started Chewing at the Zoo. It's just not my thing. But my daughter and her cousin wanted to go in there. They just needed to give the farm animals some love.

Once we actually got into the enclosure, my daughter chickened out and didn't really want to touch the animals after all. But, she did still want to *see* them up close.

Oh T-Shirt That the Goat Started Chewing at the Zoo, I should've kept a better eye on you; I will carry the guilt with me always! But how, how was I to know that while my attention was directed at the sheep two feet ahead sitting coyly on the neat straw bale, a goat would approach from behind and take a fancy to you.

It might have taken a minute for me to really notice the goat, if I'm totally honest with both of us here. I was very distracted by the contented look on my daughter's face. But as I felt the tugging getting more pronounced, I had to find out what was causing you to tighten around my waist so suddenly.

I have heard that goats eat anything, but I wasn't truly aware of the sweeping extent of this statement until I witnessed it firsthand for myself on another occasion at this very zoo. I watched as to my horror, a goat literally ate the poo as it was falling, bean by rapid fire bean, out of another goat's bum. It was not terribly unlike a frozen yogurt dispenser, only it was tiny balls of turd.

Of course you understand this is not something I can unsee. I'm talking permanent damage here. Therefore, as this particular goat's indiscriminate mandibles closed upon you, I wasn't able to ascertain with any degree of certainty that the very item he'd consumed prior to his nibblefest on your unfortunate strands of cotton wasn't a similar snack of fecal origin. I also wasn't too terribly confident that once he'd finished gorging himself on the last of your shreds he wasn't going to start on my skin as the second course. So, T-shirt That the Goat Started Chewing at the Zoo, I panicked. Given the history here, surely you must forgive my jitteriness.

Since I didn't want to get into a fight with an animal with horns and hooves, instinct took over and the only way I could see out of the situation was to literally get out of the situation. I am embarrassed to admit it, but admit it I must. There were shrieking sounds ringing out in the corral and I know they had to have been emanating from me. I put my hands on you with the intention of ripping you off and leaving the goat to munch you into oblivion, and running, with my bewildered child and nephew tucked under each arm, out of the petting zoo enclosure.

Luckily for all of us, as I began my escape maneuver one of the zoo employees noticed this scene unfolding, and she rushed over to intervene. I have no idea what the Oregon Zoo policy is regarding grown women dashing about their grounds without shirts, but I can only imagine that sort of activity is incongruent with the wholesome, family image they portray in their marketing collateral.

I could almost feel your indignity as the goat slobber slowly dried over the next few hours as we walked around from exhibit to exhibit. I could sense how angry you were with me but it was out of my hands, T-shirt That the Goat Started Chewing at the Zoo. I have washed you many times since this particular blight in your service but the scars run deep and every time I see you I am reminded of how close we came to parting on such dastardly terms.

T-shirt That the Goat Started Chewing at the Zoo, we are both but the victims here. Shall we just call a truce and move on?

Hopefully yours,
Romi

DEAR KALE

Dear Kale,

You have such a superiority complex. I suppose you are sort of a celebrity these days, you're everywhere. Sautéed kale, kale chips, roasted kale, kale flavored tea, baby kale salad, kale muffins, kale soup, kale kale…

I suppose with all the hype it must be easy to start thinking you're the next best thing since sliced bread, although, that's actually no longer the case anyway since bread contains gluten, which everyone knows is the devil and is unravelling the very fabric of our society.

Well, I have a secret to tell you. I don't like you, Kale. I don't like your thick, chewy leaves. I've never eaten burnt flubber but if I did, I imagine it would taste a lot like you.

Do I dislike you just *because* you're such a big deal these days? Just to be different? I'm not sure. All I know is I don't need to see you in EVERYTHING I eat. I miss the good old days when salads were simply salads, when I could take a bite of anything and not pick up your crunchy bits all the time.

I know you're a nutritional powerhouse, Kale. I know you are packed with vitamins. But I hate fads. I don't know why people can't just add things to their diets without going completely overboard. Couldn't you sidle up next to the spinach or broccoli quietly and add to the meal without completely ousting every other green and making such a scene? You're such a narcissist.

I will eat you sometimes, Kale, because you're good for me. I won't poison my children against you because they tolerate you as well. And actually my sister in law made some homemade kale chips that were pretty good, although I'll never admit that to you if you ever bring it up.

But I have my eye on you, Kale, I'm watching you. One day you will cease to be such a big deal and you'll be coldly replaced with the next trendy superfood.

Oh, and when you go, please take those ridiculous skinny jeans with you.

Leerily,
Romi

DEAR JEANS

Dear Jeans,

I am so sorry but I just can't anymore. I've tried so hard to stay faithful to you but I can't allow myself to let you keep hurting me like this.

I remember when we met; you were crisp and amply indigoed and hugged my curves so beautifully. Ah, I have to admit I get nostalgic as I think about how you almost touched the bottom of my platforms but held back that inch so that you lengthened my leg without soaking up all the water as we traversed the Portland rain puddles together.

You were my go-to; I could dress you up with boots and a cute sweater or slop around with you on the weekends over tennis shoes and a fleece. We were like cupcakes and frosting, weren't we, Jeans?

And then I had a baby. And another baby. I really thought we could make it work. I honestly thought I would shrink back down and could introduce you to the kids. How, Jeans, how could I possibly have known that my stomach would turn into a permanent bowl of jello.

Jeans, the times I had to lie down to button you up and almost passed out trying to suck in the flabalanche, and imagine how it stung: you dug me in the belly button in return.

Now that I think about it, you were always a little uptight after the wash and only relaxed after a wear or two. I just couldn't see the warning signs.

So I think we have reached an impasse. You can't make me happy anymore, Jeans. Your unyielding, rigid ways have come between us. I can't subject myself to heels anymore either, and your now too long pant legs are literally fraying at the edges like our torn relationship.

It pains me to tell you this, but…I have found a new love. Yes Jeans, I have been wearing Yoga Pants exclusively these days. She is flexible and comfortable and accepts me for the mom I am. Her legs flare ever so slightly so she still flatters my newfound dumpiness, but it's the fold over waist band, the WAIST BAND, Jeans, that really won me over. Once I folded the stretchy-but-not-elasticated soft knit back over itself for the first time and didn't pop an immediate muffin top, I think I actually moaned a little in ecstasy.

Please don't take it personally, Jeans. It's not you, it's me. I have changed, Jeans, and I can't ever come back. I'll even wash you one last time before I donate you to the thrift shop. Please don't make this harder on both of us, you can't have me back so let's not go there. I just can't be that uncomfortable anymore.

All the best to you my blue friend,
Romi

DEAR CUP OF TEA THAT I'LL NEVER FINISH

Dear Cup of Tea That I'll Never Finish,

No, no, it's REALLY not you. Please don't feel self-conscious for one minute. You are nothing less than perfect; hot, leafy flavor with just the right granules of sugar, and the exact splash of milk.

I love you, can't you see, you silly cup? But you and I were never destined to have our dance. All we have are stolen sips as I hide behind the cabinet, flattened against the wood so that nobody can see me. I risk it all so that I can at least sample your perfection before our time is cut short.

You are just a wisp, a tease, and damn if you aren't worth every second of the slight scalding as the sips turn to glugs when I realized I am being summoned.

You see, Cup of Tea That I'll Never Finish, I won't ever see the bottom of your mug. I know this even as I take the hopeful bag out of the canister, as I boil the water, as I stir the sugar and milk, as I hold the spoon in my hand while I try to drink you because the clink of the metal hitting the sink would just part us even sooner.

Cup of Tea That I'll Never Finish, the harsh reality is that while I want you with all my soul, it's out of my hands. As soon as my children find out I am going to sit with you and enjoy your luscious warmth for a minute, they find things that require my immediate and desperate attention. It will always be this way. We are but the Romeo and Juliet of hot beverages and drinkers.

While you cool to your tepid death on the counter, I will be having a heated argument about a stuffed lamb toy with a three-year-old, or cleaning peanut butter stains off the wall. There will be broken glass, spilled juice, socks that don't match, a guitar that lost one of its strings, a wiggly tooth that is getting its last whiplash inside a gum.

But regardless of what it is that causes our divorce each time, Cup of Tea That I'll Never Finish, I wanted you to know that it's simply our circumstances, it's not personal. I will still brew you, just in case. After all, hope springs eternal.

Yours,
Romi

DEAR TO ERASE AND RERECORD PLEASE PRESS THREE

Dear To Erase and Rerecord Please Press Three,

I am deeply indebted to you, sweet guardian angel of voice recording flubs and verbal diarrhea.

Why it is that I am seemingly incapable of leaving a succinct, clear voicemail message the first time – or third – is sadly beyond me. All I know is that halfway into a two minute and twenty second harangue on someone's poor unsuspecting voicemail box, I am calmed and relieved to remember that after the desperately long-winded monologue you will be there to bail me out.

You patiently allow me to reinvent myself as many times as it takes for me to basically tell someone to please call me back in five hundred words or less. You do not judge.

Oh, To Erase and Rerecord Please Press Three, you are the patron saint of my advanced case of blarney stone-itis.

It hasn't always been chocolate and roses though, right, To Erase and Rerecord Please Press Three? You may think I've forgotten, but I still remember the indignity of those times when I warbled on, digging myself into a chasm of articulation strangulation, stumbling and umming like a fool, until finally I stopped and pressed the pound sign, only to hear the silence of the still–recording message running in the background. In a frantic attempt to hear your kind offer, I even tried pressing the number one button, but alas, the recording rolled on.

Yes, To Erase and Rerecord Please Press Three, those were dark days, but we have moved on. For the most part, on a typical day, you are all that stands between me making a complete donkey of myself and the predominantly professional messages that I deposit on answering machines all over the free world.

Thank you, To Erase and Rerecord Please Press Three. Beautiful miracle that you are, you are a technological life jacket and I will cling to you devotedly.

Gratefully,
Romi

DEAR TOO OLD TO DO PORN BUT NEED

A LITTLE EXTRA CASH

Dear Too Old to do Porn but Need a Little Extra Cash,

Well that's a bummer. Sort of. I mean, I didn't seriously have any intention of doing porn to begin with and pregnancy really did a number on my body, so I can't imagine anyone would want to pay to see it performing in such a manner anyway. But, it does seem to be such an easy ticket for a little extra dough from time to time.

Sure, there's always getting a second job, or peddling wares on handmade online market places, or reselling clothes and other used crap to people who actually want to buy other people's crap.

But it just seems it would take so much longer to make the same amount of money.

And even though I couldn't really do it since I'm too washed up, Too Old to do Porn but Need a Little Extra Cash, it would be nice to have the *option* of doing it if I *wanted to*. It's always nice to have choices, don't you think?

My husband insists that no matter what the fetish, someone out there would pay to see it. There are apparently people who get off on watching people in high heels pop balloons, or stomp on cockroaches. (Or perhaps he made all that up??)

Regardless, I think this bag of bones and jello just isn't marketable. I don't think there's a fetish for this.

Sigh. I guess that kitchen remodel will just have to wait.

Bow chicka wow wow...

Romi

DEAR POTTY THAT SCARED THE CRAP OUT OF MY CHILD

Dear Potty That Scared the Crap out of My Child,

Oh, the irony. If only you actually would.

My son is nearly four now, Potty That Scared the Crap out of My Child, and it's getting to be that time. Well no, it's way past that time but you see, thanks to the fearful and terrifying piece of equipment that you are, we are as close to potty training our youngster as we are to being able to build a rocket out of the empty diaper boxes we've amassed and fly to Jupiter.

Our intentions were good. Like all parents, and especially second-timers, we knew potty training would be a struggle. We bought you, all cute and shiny, a miniature version of our own toilet, designed specifically for the miniature version of my husband and myself who was destined to make your acquaintance.

Potty That Scared the Crap out of My Child, when we took you out of the box, my son began to shriek and ran away. He was appalled! Instead of being amused by your fun pretend handle or thinking your perfectly small-bummed size bowl was as amazing as Christmas morning, he dissolved into a flurry of tears and disappeared into a very remote corner of the house to do his business. In his diaper.

How could you be so insensitive? How could you just sit there quietly exuding such torment from your cheerily stickered happy face while my son recoiled in horror? We talked you up, Potty That Scared the Crap out of My Child. We invested some serious time into telling our youngster how amazing you were. And yet, you only served to be a complete and utter petrifying disappointment.

Now you take your place in the potty hall of shame, the place in our home where all the other potties and training seats have gone to die. As the dust gathers on your nightmare-inducing exterior, another diaper gets its wings, and another and another.

Thanks for nothing, you turd burgler.

Romi

DEAR OBSESSION WITH STATS

Dear Obsession with Stats,

Please forgive me but I just don't see it. What is your actual contribution to corporate life and society in general?

There are so many hours spent on you, Obsession with Stats. There are people whose sole job it is to track you down to the nearest hundredth of a point, to know to the nth power exactly how many widgets were sold, how many people were happy to be selling the widgets, if they were 3.673% happier or not as happy to be selling the widgets as they were last year, if they feel their management communicated to them effectively enough about widget sales in general, if the company vision of widget sales is crystally clear, if the customers who buy the widgets think these are the most mind-blowingly fantastic widgets they've ever seen, to project how many widgets they think will sell next year and make sure the employees sell them, would rather continue selling them for THIS company or leave to sell them for someone else, what percentage of employees think they're not paid enough to sell the widgets, what number of employees felt their voices weren't heard adequately in the planning of widget sales, how much productivity is being lost by employees who manufacture widgets going to the bathroom or eating their lunch or saying good morning to fellow employees at the office each day.

Good God, Obsession with Stats!

Can't we just treat our employees nicely and then feel secure knowing they're happy in their jobs? Can't we just get our work done and have the satisfaction of knowing we're being productive?

Do we have to waste half the day pulling you and messing around with you in fancy spreadsheets to make you look pretty so that we can try and figure out why we don't have enough time to do our actual jobs?

No offense, but I think you've just taken it 87.93% too far, Obsession with Stats.

Romi

DEAR WRINKLES

Dear Wrinkles,

While I knew I would eventually make your acquaintance, I was admittedly a little shocked when you showed up in my thirties. THIRTIES, Wrinkles, come on!

As is the nature of such things, at first I was in denial that you were there. Surely it was just my imagination. Yet almost overnight I went from being that person who always got carded to being asked if I was my husband's mother. Finally when my daughter started drawing pictures of me with lines on my forehead rivaling that of a shar-pei, I could no longer pretend I still looked like I had fallen into the fountain of youth.

I endeavored not to panic but rather conduct a scientific, honest assessment of my apparently increasingly crumpled epidermis. As I peered into the mirror, so close that my breath fogged up the glass and in fact made you disappear quite nicely, there was no denying your crinkled presence on my previously flawless skin.

As I stared even closer, eyeball to glass, I noticed you had been at work for a while, etching little lines all over my forehead and skating from the corners of my eyes towards my hairline. These were startling enough;

however, the most distressing observation of all was the deep, almost chiseled trenches that ran from the outsides of my nose down my cheeks.

Then I have to say, I got a little angry. Sure, I suppose I could have used sunblock all those blissful summers but it was the '80s, Wrinkles, everyone was doing it.

After having babies did things to my body that no person so young has any business with, my face was all I had left, you see. Not that I stopped traffic, Wrinkles, let's be honest with ourselves here, but it was all I had. And you wrecked it. So yes, I was pretty unhappy with you for a while.

And then a remarkable thing happened. I found out that in order to leave a visible wrinkle, a muscle has to make that movement ten thousand times. Whoa! This changed everything. I got out the magnification mirror and had another good long look at you while I made faces at myself in the reflection.

And I got it.

With every smile, you sprang to life, even more exaggerated than before. When you fanned out from each eyelid in a spectacular display of crows feet, I realized that was when my eyes were at their twinkliest.

It also didn't escape my attention that I have no frown lines yet, a pretty reassuring reminder that I have spent more time cheerful than tearful.

So it turns out you're not so much a collection of blots on the Custer's last stand that was my face but a living museum of tens of thousands of smiles and countless more thousands of peals of laughter. I think I can live with that.

So I forgive you, Wrinkles. Thank you for a fun ride. Just stay away from my neck.

Romi

DEAR WHAT I FEARED WAS A SPIDER ON MY NECK BUT THANK GOD IT WAS JUST DRIED SNOT

Dear What I Feared Was a Spider on my Neck but Thank God it was Just Dried Snot,

This was it. The defining moment that has made me feel like a mother like none other before. See, it was a crisp, autumn day. It had been pouring for a week, so when we had a break in the rain I knew I had to make hay while the sun shone (as they say in the motherland) and rake the leaves that had blanketed my driveway in a thick, orange-brown carpet of sog.

We only had about an hour before sunset. I asked the kids if they wanted to come out and help me and without hesitation, both of my little pumpkins volunteered merrily. We donned our coats and boots and hurried for the door; rakes, brooms and electric leaf vac in hand.

My girl got down to business right away and a large pile of leaves swelled magnificently at the bottom of the driveway. My boy attacked the stretch where the cul de sac met the driveway with equal fervor. All was going so well!

But then, What I Feared Was a Spider on my Neck but Thank God it was Just Dried Snot, my boy became bored. He wandered off, returning seconds later with a gigantic set of shears that I use for cutting small branches; a set of shears that is longer than the boy himself, and capable of dismembering fingers and possibly small hands from their wrists. He staggered towards the hedge that lines the edge of the driveway with the aforementioned weapon.

I threw down my broom and zipped over there as fast as my legs could carry me. I explained that little boys have no business with such equipment and told him to relinquish it immediately. He didn't think too much of my idea and began bargaining. I asked if he wanted to go inside then, and with that he flung the shears onto the ground and ran over to my car in a flurry of tears. He flung the door open, jumped up inside and with a dramatic flourish, slammed it shut.

I picked up the electric leaf vac and began vacuuming the straggler leaves. I am not the most gifted person in the hearing department as it is, and definitely couldn't hear anything over the roar of the motor.

So when I switched off the leaf blower after about five minutes to empty the bag, the sound of my poor son's unmistakable shrieks rang out like a bell and reverberated round and round the cul de sac.

Bolting over to the car, I threw the door open to find a very shaken and penitent boy weeping in the back seat. I pulled him into my arms and he nestled into my neck. Between gasping breaths and stuttering sobs, he informed me that he had been unable to open the door himself.

The poor boy, What I Feared Was a Spider on my Neck but Thank God it was Just Dried Snot. This really concerned me since of course it's imperative that someone his age knows how to open a car door if he is ever trapped inside and needs to get out. I gave him a lesson in car door opening 101 right there on the spot.

I gave him the warmest hug I could, and covered his ruddy little face with kisses. The three of us finished up our raking expedition and high tailed it back inside the house as darkness fell over the neighborhood.

It was time to begin preparing dinner. As I pored over my cookbook, deciding what to make, my hand absently went up to my neck. I felt you there, hard and kind of crunchy, and, having just been outside, my first inclination was to assume there was a bug on my neck.

I peeled you off and flung you on the counter, my heart pounding wildly. I did the obligatory frenzied shaking out of my hair in case there were more in there, but didn't feel anything. Somewhat satisfied that I had found all there was to find, I scrutinized you on the tiles for a minute, breathing shallowly.

You were curled up in the manner of spiders who are no longer of this world; their spindly legs curled in towards their bodies. I had to really peer closely to rule out that you definitely *weren't* a spider, but where the body would be, a blob of indeterminate shape took its place.

I felt the cold wave of relief wash over me, a strange mix with the adrenaline, What I Feared Was a Spider on my Neck but Thank God it was Just Dried Snot. You were NOT a spider after all, but just snot that must have transferred onto me and then dried, after I hugged my bereft child in the car that afternoon.

And then a reckoning came over me in the next wave. The fact was, not only was having someone else's snot on my own skin not even repulsive, but I was actually genuinely GLAD that's what you were, as opposed to the alternative.

Astounding. This, I decided, THIS above all else, is what it means to be a mother.

Maternally yours,
Romi

DEAR SHOWER THAT I DARED TO HAVE ALONE

Dear Shower That I Dared to Have Alone,

You must know I dream of you. I am ashamed to say I took you for granted back when I could have you all the time, but now I know better.

Don't get me wrong. The life I have chosen was my choice and is my bliss, I wouldn't have it any other way. And truth to tell, trying to cleanse myself while the door flies open two hundred times and people walk in and out of the bathroom used to sound like an outrageous violation of my privacy but I hardly even notice it anymore.

That is until, like a junkie who just can't stay away, I find my way back to you, Shower That I Dared to Have Alone. Sometimes I must have you and I don't care at what cost.

Sometimes I just need to feel the water running as hot as it can go without having to worry about making it cooler so as not to burn little hands that throw open the door and fling themselves under the stream. To take a moment to breathe and finish a thought before a little voice asks a question to interrupt it.

I once saw "bath" as an option on a spa package and wondered what idiot would spend fifty bucks to go somewhere else and sit in a bath. Now I am an idiot of such. Now I get it.

You must understand, we cannot make a habit of this. Shhhh, it's okay, it's okay. There will be many days once my children are grown that we will meet daily. But now they need me, Shower That I Dared to Have Alone. I must be there for them. Even with shampoo running into my eyes while I explain again why I have stretchmarks or why my bellybutton looks sad. Even as the lights are going on and off and on and off and a herd of three-inch pachyrhinosauruses are waging war outside the glass. Even when I lock the door to the bathroom on occasion but they pick the lock anyway.

Wait for me, Shower That I Dared to Have Alone. I will long for you desperately.

Clandestinely yours. Always.

Romi

DEAR WAKING UP FOR A FIVE THIRTY AM MEETING ONLY TO LOG IN AND FIND IT'S BEEN CANCELLED

Dear Waking Up for a Five Thirty AM Meeting Only to Log in and Find It's Been Cancelled, Oh COME ON NOW. Did you hear what I said? FIVE THIRTY.

I got out of bed at that time of the morning for you, bumbled downstairs in the inky darkness while the rest of the West coast was still sawing logs and nearly gave myself a laceration from standing on the tiny plastic sheep that was left on the stairs the night before.

I may have cursed a few times on my way to my desk but I did it. I came downstairs.

With bleary eyes that stubbornly refused to focus properly, I switched on my laptop. I put in the first thousand passwords and waited. The laptop came to life as sluggishly as I had and finally I logged into Outlook.

And there it was, Happy Wednesday to me. The hole on my calendar where you'd been just the night before. Waking Up for a Five Thirty AM Meeting Only to Log in and Find It's Been Cancelled, I didn't need this. Every minute of sleep is sacred. You April-fooling-when-it's-not-even-April-sleep-dashing-sadist, I have children who keep me awake all hours of the night. In a fantastic twist of irony, this particular morning my two cherubs were actually still asleep at that ungodly hour, but it was you this time. YOU who woke me up for nothing.

Thaaaaaaaaaaaaaanks,

Romi

DEAR LAST BITE OF MANGO THAT FELL

ON THE FLOOR

Dear Last Bite of Mango that Fell on the Floor,

Why? WHY, you complete disappointment? I'd picked out the mango earlier that day at the store. It was a rare special treat that I was going to let myself have. See, I'm on a new eating plan these days, and even a mango is probably too much sugar but for the love of biscuits, I have to live a *little*.

And in case you didn't notice, you have to exert yourself to eat a fruit like this. This isn't an apple you just wash and chomp. It's not a banana that you easily peel and enjoy. Mangoes are more of a commitment. You have to invest some time, Last Bite of Mango that Fell on the Floor, before you reap the fruit of your labor, so to speak.

There's the peeling of the skin, the careful carving of the gorgeous school bus yellow flesh, the cutting of the fruit into bite size pieces, the veritable river of mango juice running down your hands and elbows into your sleeves to mop up.

But it's worth it Last Bite of Mango that Fell on the Floor. It's worth it to me to practically follow a twelve-step program just to have a mango, because I LOVE them. Because, when I'm eating one, for a just a moment, no matter what nonsense has come my way during the day, I can concentrate on the heavenly taste and have a quiet, religious experience.

As the pieces start to dwindle and I know my time with this magic produce is getting short, every bite counts.

So imagine my irritation and resentment when I picked you up with the fork, Last Bite of Mango that Fell on the Floor, and you plummeted to the kitchen tile next to my left foot. My last bite. The finale, the culmination of the culinary excursion I had just taken. I had such hopes for you. And then you were gone. Well worse than that really, you were wasted.

I suppose this letter will have to be closure then, a hollow attempt to satisfy the snack summit that will never be.

Glumly,
Romi

DEAR BAND AID THAT HAD THE

WRONG PICTURE ON IT

Dear Band Aid That Had the Wrong Picture on it,

What can I say? Part of it is really my fault because when my child has a cut on his finger, my motherly instinct is just to stop the bleeding as soon as possible.

It wasn't a terrible laceration or anything, just your standard kid scrape. But as you must have been forewarned before going into your line of work, children can tend to get a *teeny* tiny bit dramatic (read: completely hysterical as if the affected area is going to fall off) when they see a hint of red appearing at the site of the cut.

Sometimes as you are probably also aware, there may not even be any evidence of the alleged injury that is visible without the assistance of a microscope, but the universe can nevertheless come to a complete standstill in this situation until you are neatly applied.

It's part of the ritual, you see, Band Aid That Had the Wrong Picture on it. My child hurt himself and began shrieking. I came to his aid to find him writhing in pain, holding the wound. When I attempted to see the wound so that I could determine what kind of first aid needed to be applied, my child recoiled and bellowed at me NOT TO TOUCH IT! It was then my job to convince the boy that I was not going to touch it, just look at it. Reluctantly he removed his hands to reveal the abrasion.

There were actual blood droplets this time so I felt you were warranted, Band Aid That Had the Wrong Picture on it. I moved quickly, spraying on the Bactine to ease the sting and disinfect the area and then fished you out of the box.

Again, through no fault of your own, I couldn't clearly see your design through the paper casing. Of course I knew you were perfectly suited to the job, Band Aid That Had the Wrong Picture on it, and I knew that your cosmetic overcoat didn't matter at all, as long as you concealed my son's boo boo.

But I'm not a three-year-old.

In your further defense, the boy didn't even articulate which particular design he wanted to have save the day, but as with all things, mothers are supposed to read their children's minds and anticipate their every need and whim.

So I can imagine how embarrassing it was for you, Band Aid That Had the Wrong Picture on it, when I applied you to the cut and my son insisted that you come straight off. Your adhesive hadn't even had a chance to bond properly with the skin yet, you hadn't even had a chance to serve and protect, and he sentenced you to go.

I was dismayed and told him it didn't matter, that (and sorry but I had to use this for effect here) you're all just as good as the others. But he wasn't buying it at all.

We were in public you see, Band Aid That Had the Wrong Picture on it, and besides making sure our children are safe, a mother's job is also to make sure that we minimize scenes and outbursts to the best of our ability.

This is not just a matter of saving our own eardrums; the existence of all humankind is at stake here! If too many childless people witness tantrums over various things like band aids that are not up to snuff, they may opt out of having children themselves! It may be the most effective form of contraception ever! BandAid That Had the Wrong Picture on it, DO YOU REALLY WANT ME TO BE RESPONSIBLE FOR THE FALL OF THE HUMAN SPECIES?! I didn't think so. It was a service for the greater good.

I ripped you off and sent you to your doom too soon, it was before your time. But I did what I had to do. You were so brave. I then replaced you with three identically sized band aids who were so unceremoniously sent to their deaths as well, and then finally applied the fourth that did exactly as you would have, had your artwork been more acceptable. It soaked up the blood droplets and then as fast as the banshee wailing began, it subsided, letting my son get back to his day; the whole thing forgotten faster than the tears could evaporate from his lashes.

Miraculous.

Thanks for trying,

Romi

DEAR ARMS

Dear Arms,

I am ashamed to say I spent so many years hating you. You are short and thick, with plenty of insulation from your rounded shoulders to the chubby pads of your thickset fingers.

For so long I hid you in long sleeved shirts, even in the blistery heat of summer, because you weren't lithe and square, long and sleek; you weren't perfect, like you were supposed to be.

Arms, recently I had breakfast with a good friend. She is beautiful, full of life and effervescent energy, with sparkly eyes and a gorgeous smile. She has the sort of long, square-shouldered arms I always thought you should be, and yet, unprompted and out of the blue, she told me that she always wanted her arms to be more like YOU!

She said that no matter how I moved, your muscles popped up; that she could see definition and shape within you that she wished she had in her own arms! I was floored. I was so focused on the squishy bits that I had never been able to see that about you, and yet, she is correct. You do have lots of muscle, and if I was to stop judging you so harshly for a minute I would see it, and moreover, appreciate it.

Oh Arms, I am so sorry. You have rocked my babies to sleep, and held them when they were scared. You pushed them on the swings, danced with them in the living room, and held the sprinkler for them while they ran through it, shrieking with delight. You hugged them tightly when they needed the kind of love that only a mother can give.

Your veins have afforded blood donations for those whose lives lie perilously in the balance; you have steered the wheel of the car on countless adventures. You have helped my children turn household scraps into priceless artwork and planted gardens of magnificent flowers.

You have been so hard at work every day for forty years, quietly doing my every bidding without ever so much as an appreciative thought, to say nothing of a thank you.

Welcome back to the sunlight, Arms. I cannot muster up the energy to hate you any longer or care if other people do as well. I will not sequester you away in any more stuffy shifts or suffocating wraps. I will proudly show you to the world, flab and all, and if people are offended by the sight of you then frankly that's their own damn problem, and they can look away.

Now if you don't mind, I need to go have a word with some friends of yours, Legs. It seems that sadly I have mistreated them in the same way, and I need to absolve them of the crimes that I have so ridiculously heaped upon them for no other reason than my own pettiness.

Be well, my dear Arms. I hope you will forgive me for my selfish neglect so that we can both move on together. In a cool, cotton tank top of course.

Lots of love,

Romi

DEAR VANILLA

Dear Vanilla,

You poor, misunderstood bean. You have somehow become synonymous with all that is blah and bland and basic, but they've got it hopelessly wrong.

You are magnificent! I am madly in love with your delicate, complex flavor and I use you like an addict at every possible opportunity. If it's any consolation, I want you to know you are my secret baking weapon; the ingredient I always add even if the recipe doesn't want you to play in the mixing bowl. Because you just make everything better.

Even waffles and chocolate chip cookies need your benevolent essence to give them some magic. And then, Vanilla, the very mouths that devour those molten confections for which you so lovingly lay down your life, deprecate you in the next mouthful with their condescending putdowns and disparaging sneers.

And yet, make fun of you as they might, you are the base sweet aroma in the candle aisle at Target, the candle I always come back to, to try and get the stench of pine or worse, ghastly fake cinnamon out of my nostrils.

They even put you in tea. Which, sorry, is an abomination, as tea should be plain with milk and a little sugar (YES! I said the s-word), but that's not your fault, Vanilla.

They are jealous of you, my sweet Cinderella, but fear not. You can come to my ball anytime.

Loyally,
Romi

DEAR TINY TURQUOISE BEADS THAT MY TODDLER FOUND

Dear Tiny Turquoise Glass Beads that My Toddler Found,

You really should have known better. Sitting there in the jar all shiny and gleaming, just beckoning to such a small boy to come and knock you over. You *had* to know that you were basically a double dog dare to my child to pull the stool over and nearly scrape the skin off his legs trying to scale the countertop to get to you.

How could a small boy possibly resist shoving his little hands into the jar to squish you between his fingers and fling handfuls of you around the bathroom?

Tiny Turquoise Glass Beads that My Toddler Found, the thing is, we were just preparing to put our house on the market. There was a lot going on, you see, we had to upgrade some of the flooring and put in new light fixtures, we had to replace some things that were a bit worn and grubby and make sure the house was immaculate.

We even rented a storage unit to move all our overflowing crap off the premises so our property that houses a family of four could look like nobody lives in it.

Of course there is the small matter of the house inspection, Tiny Turquoise Glass Beads that My Toddler Found, so everything has to be in perfect working order. Enticing my boy to spill half of you down into the drain of the sink really didn't help our confidence level that all would go well at the aforementioned event.

And possibly the best part: how could you have led my toddler to pour the remaining half of you into the reed diffuser bottle?! Once he'd mixed you up with the vanilla oil, he poured the newly blended creation all over the countertops. Oil on the tile grout, Tiny Turquoise Glass Beads that My Toddler Found. I need not tell you how enjoyable of an experience that cleanup was.

The other matter I have to discuss with you is the ingestion factor. Tiny Turquoise Glass Beads that My Toddler Found, do you know I had to finally take my toddler to the doctor because he had been eating bark chips on such frequent occasions? If he eats bark chips, sand dollars and Legos, how on earth was he supposed to resist your smooth and delectable texture?

Really, Tiny Turquoise Glass Beads that My Toddler Found, that was just sneaky.

Unimpressed,
Romi

DEAR INOPPORTUNE CATERPILLAR IN

MY DAUGHTER'S ARTICHOKE

Dear Inopportune Caterpillar in My Daughter's Artichoke,

Why, you unfortunate bastard? Why, of all artichokes, of all dinner plates for all children, did you have to end up in that one?

You see, Inopportune Caterpillar in My Daughter's Artichoke, my daughter doesn't like to eat her vegetables. It's been a real struggle, honestly, to get her to eat anything green. We have tried so many things, from charts to having her pick them out at the store, from helping me cook them to even growing them. She has tried so hard, she truly has, but she just doesn't dig them.

But artichokes. These were the leafy promised land, the ones she ate willingly and happily, plucking each petal from the gigantic bulb and dipping it gingerly in the butter before scraping the delicious crescent of meat from its edges. Yes of course it's mostly the butter that got her attention, Inopportune Caterpillar in My Daughter's Artichoke, but that's not the point. She did actually reap some of the benefits of the veggie itself in amongst the unsalted sweet cream prop.

On the fateful night in question, she was blissfully making her way through her side dish when she noticed a telltale groove carved into one of the petals. She examined it more carefully, her eye travelling along the rut, squinting more and more closely until she finally squealed, "UGH! Is that a CATERPILLAR?!"

I was all set to deny it, to say it wasn't so, and yet when I peered more closely I had to concur. There you were, embedded in the side, mere inches from her fingers.

In fairness to you, being steamed alive while you were innocently munching on this cherished, not to mention *expensive* vegetable, is not a fate I'd wish upon my worst enemy, Inopportune Caterpillar in my Daughter's Artichoke. Going by way of the larvae version of death by old faithful must have been awful, God rest your wriggly, ill-fated soul.

However, now my girl is done, you see. I can't predict when it is that she will ever touch another artichoke, but I know it won't happen again for a long, looooong time. Sadder yet, I know it will be a good long while before she eats *any* other veggie now, at least without putting up a fight that will leave both her and me feeling frustrated and depleted.

She refused to eat a pear today, her favorite fruit, as she was worried about meeting one of your friends in there, Inopportune Caterpillar in My Daughter's Artichoke. She also pushed the bowl of apple sauce away, saying she just couldn't stomach its contents. And I'm sure we haven't even got started yet. Even with my most putrid math skills, when I showed her that she has been ingesting fruits and veggies for almost three thousand days and only come up against one caterpillar, thereby making the odds of finding another one in her food so negligibly small it's almost impossible, she still wasn't having any of it.

So thank you very much you miserably timed and ruinous half inch destroyer of good eating habits. In fifteen seconds, you decimated what my daughter and I had spent the last eight years building. "Five a day" just fell off the wagon and gave itself a concussion.

In frustration,
Romi

DEAR AIRLINES THEY SHOULD HAVE THAT JUST CATER TO PEOPLE WITH KIDS

Dear Airlines They Should Have That Just Cater to People with Kids,

How I wish you were real! I can see it now, a plane where babies can cry as loudly as they like when their little ears hurt, where toddlers can jump up and sit down and stand and sit and wriggle and squiggle and stand and sit. For HOURS.

Where there is a false row of seats, a façade really, in between every REAL row of seats, for little children to kick to their hearts' content without making the people sitting in front of them lose their minds.

Ah, Airlines They Should Have That Just Cater to People with Kids, your snacks would be Goldfish crackers and grapes, blueberries and yogurt squeezers instead of the savory pretzel sticks that children won't eat, and you would just bring them continuously.

I can imagine the back of the plane, not crammed with seats but an open place where, if the fasten seatbelt light is turned off, kids could bring their dinosaurs and Legos, their dolls and cars and just play for a while.

Airlines They Should Have That Just Cater to People with Kids, how great would it be if your seats reclined so that our kids, beside themselves with exhaustion and boredom from being confined for so long, could stretch out and actually sleep. You would have toilets where the sound and ferocity of the flush wouldn't scare children, and their parents could help their youngsters without needing an Olympic gold medal in acrobatics to fit in the bathroom with them.

Your lounges at the airport wouldn't be for first class passengers but rather very important teeny people, a safe enclosed space where the tiny jetset could play and burn off some energy before boarding.

Your tray tables would have raised edges so that all those crayons and toys didn't keep rolling off the edge.

Airlines They Should Have but Don't That Just Cater to People with Kids, I would pay extra for you. Oh yes, I would pay.

Dreamily,
Romi

DEAR LINE TO SEE THE PONY THAT WE GOT IN AND OUT AND IN AND OUT AND IN

Dear Line to See the Pony that We Got In and Out and In and Out and In,

The thing is, I'm not sure my boy would have wanted to ride the pony at all if his sister wasn't so keen to go herself. We were at the pumpkin patch, having eaten three bites of hotdog, several ears of corn, honey sticks and two bites of caramel apples. The pumpkins had been chosen, our bodies thoroughly shaken by the bumpy hayride, and we were actually on our way out.

And then my girl saw the ponies. It was all over then you understand, Line to See the Pony that We Got In and Out and In and Out and In. My girl loves to ride on the ponies and it was now a done deal.

I asked my son if he wanted to ride a pony as well. He shook his head emphatically and assured me he didn't. I bought one ticket. While no fault of your own, you weren't a short wait.

Somewhere between no and no, my youngster decided that he did in fact want to ride on a horsey. I bought a second ticket. But as luck would have it, he wanted the little brown pony that had already been set into service by a girl ahead of him by two spaces.

My girl took her place on a larger pony and then it was my boy's turn. Of course as diminutive, kindly-looking Twinkle approached the starting point, my boy wanted none of it.

The owner of the pony show and I tried to coax him into giving it a try, but he was done by that point.

The owner very sweetly refunded my money and we stood to the side, watching my girl serenely going round and round the pen.

Of course now this looked really fun so my son decided he had erred and asked to go.

We took our place in line again. Again we whiled away the minutes, during which time my boy changed his mind back and forth several more times.

We approached the front of the line and then he hmmm'ed and hah'ed again over the selection of diminutive steeds. The pony lady had clearly had her fill of us. She took my boy and just plonked him on top of the brown one.

He looked quite horrified at first, Line to See the Pony that We Got In and Out and In and Out and In, but then relaxed as he started going round in their straw-strewn orbit. The highlight of the whole experience was when the pony in front of him lifted his tail and demonstrated to my child at very close range how animals of its ilk dispose of the remains of their lunch.

Excellent.

Romi

DEAR THE FIVE MINUTES OF MY CHILDREN BEING NICE TO EACH OTHER BEFORE THE SHRIEKING STARTS

Dear The Five Minutes of my Children Being Nice to Each Other Before the Shrieking Starts,

How sweet you are. In these rare, stolen snippets of time, right before my eardrums are rattled with the most earthshattering screams of unadulterated, venomous sibling rivalry, you bring me to the edge of bliss with pure, joyous love. A love so deep and huge it feels as though it will split my heart into a thousand shards of exploding happiness.

A hug perhaps, the sister's longer arms wrapped around her brother's smaller back, his head nestled on her shoulder. Or maybe a page of a story read so tenderly, a little boy in his big sister's lap, their two chestnut haired heads touching. Sometimes you are the fort they build, pillows and sheets flying back and forth over the couch; the favorite stuffed animal given to big sister to cheer her up after a disappointing day at school. Sometimes you are the sound of their giggling; chortles intermingling like a choir whose song is made of bubbles of laughter floating deliciously in the air.

And then, The Five Minutes of my Children Being Nice to Each Other Before the Shrieking Starts, you are once again the eye of the storm. Your sudden end is violently wrought as they turn on each other and your calm, lovely presence dissipates into the ethos as if you never existed.

You'll be back, at some point, although when is anyone's guess. This is the magic that you are, I suppose. You cannot be forced or artificially conjured up, you appear again organically when the time is right and the genuine moment is there.

The Five Minutes of my Children Being Nice to Each Other Before the Shrieking Starts, I love you because you symbolize hope. Despite the bickering that is characteristic of how my children typically interact with each other, as I witness your brief appearance on and off throughout the day, I know you are *possible*.

You are the seeds of the bond that will bind them; you are the lifeblood of a rare friendship they will have with no one else.

And one day when I am gone, you will help them to hold each other up. You will be *home*.

With my deepest gratitude,
Romi

ACKNOWLEDGEMENTS

Once again, my undying gratitude to Amy Hansen for editing this book and providing solid advice until it arrived at its final polished form.

To Jennifer Hall, thank you so much for being my grammar ninja and for your thoughtful and spot-on perspective.

A big thank you to Deborah Bradseth of Tugboat Design for another amazing cover design and making the process so easy.

To every reader who picked up this little number and gave it a go, thank you for your time, I hope you enjoyed it!

To all the little things in life that have ever felt unnoticed or unappreciated, here is your moment in the sun…

And, as always, a giant thank you to my family, Mom, extended family and friends, who are there for me no matter what. I love you!

We hope you enjoyed this book! Please would you consider leaving a review? Thanks so much!

Check out Romi's other books:

Please Tell Me I'm On Mute
Mommy Can We Have a Jellyfish?

For more information, find her at:

Twitter: @RomiBrennerBook
Facebook: Author Romi Brenner

www.ingramcontent.com/pod-product-compliance
Lightning Source LLC
Chambersburg PA
CBHW060533030426

42337CB00021B/4240